T0110187

# Spiritual
# Makeup
# Bag

*Discovering Beauty from the Inside Out*

Kim A. Thomas

WESTBOW
PRESS®
A DIVISION OF THOMAS NELSON
& ZONDERVAN

WestBow Press books may be ordered through booksellers or by contacting:

WestBow Press
A Division of Thomas Nelson & Zondervan
1663 Liberty Drive
Bloomington, IN 47403
www.westbowpress.com
1 (866) 928-1240

ISBN: 978-1-9736-9515-8 (sc)
ISBN: 978-1-9736-9514-1 (e)

Library of Congress Control Number: 2020911737

Print information available on the last page.

WestBow Press rev. date: 06/24/2020

To Jordan, Brittany, Emily, and Jessica, who inspired me to finish this book. I'm praying this will be a resource and reminder of the beauty inside each one of you.

"Spiritual Makeup Bag is an encouraging and inspiring reminder that true beauty begins on the inside. Kim Thomas is transparent as she shares personal stories from her own journey of discovering true beauty. You, too, can become the beautiful woman God has called you to be."

Lisa Collins, Co-founding Pastor, Church Eleven32 Allen, TX

"What a beautiful reminder of God's love. Amongst all the distractions that come with being a busy mom, wife, friend, and female entrepreneur, it's easy to get caught up our to-do list rather than chasing our true purpose according to Him. Spiritual Makeup Bag is an essential asset to any woman who seeks to recognize true meaning in our efforts as a strong female presence in this world. It serves as a reminder we can't do it all, but God can move mountains in our lives ... IF we seek Him first."

Charla Corn Barrett, CEO of Blessings Breakthrough

"Spiritual Makeup Bag is a rare and wonderfully written book that provides a practical application for women of all ages. Men can use it too! The author's unique use of women of the Bible is a fascinating resource that will keep the reader focused from start to finish. This is a book the reader will want to share with others."

Dr. Gary K. Walker, Retired College Administrator
and Author of Letters from Grandpa

Don't try to make yourselves beautiful on the outside,
with stylish hair or by wearing gold jewelry or fine clothes.
Instead, make yourselves beautiful on the inside, in your
hearts, with the enduring quality of a gentle, peaceful spirit.
This type of beauty is very precious in God's eyes.
—1 Peter 3:3–4 (CEB)

# Contents

# Chapter 1

## I Say a Little Prayer

In the morning, LORD, you hear my voice; in the morning
I lay my requests before you and wait expectantly.
—Psalm 5:3 (NIV)

I'd rather sleep than get up early and read my Bible.

There, I confessed it!

There have been times in my life when I was so desperate for God that I hopped out of bed and sought His Word.

But the truth is, most days I'd rather sleep.

Then there are those times when I read my Bible and find myself checking it off my to-do list and getting it done rather than sitting with my Lord and Savior.

For most of us, we know the right thing to do—to get up early while it's still dark and quiet and sit alone with our cup of coffee or tea and open the crisp pages of our Holy Bible. I love those mornings when I read God's Word and something in the pages jumps right off and speaks to me. When I pray before reading, God speaks to me through His Word. It's inspiring and makes me ready to *carpe diem*—a.k.a. seize the day! Psalm 5:3 helps us understand the importance of getting up and being with God.

I want the desire to get out of bed and go see what God has for me in His Word, and that's where the struggle gets real. I don't want to do it for the sake of doing it, even though I believe God can bless any act of obedience even if it's with the wrong motive. He can take reluctant followers and make them into passionate believers in Jesus Christ if they just take one simple act of faith, one step of faith, one morning of getting up and opening the Bible.

So why do I forget that feeling of fullness the next day when I don't want to get up early and read my Bible? Some might say it's a heart issue, and maybe it is, because Jeremiah 17:9 tells us that "the heart is deceitful above all things and beyond cure who can understand it."

I know that I love God and I know Jesus Christ is my Lord and Savior and I want to live for God. I know I can't live for Him without hearing from Him, and the only way to hear from Him is to spend time with Him. So I came up with an idea after thinking through my mornings and shared it in a talk. This talk was a part of the launch of our new Women's Ministry at church, and I was the speaker, which is hilarious because it was my first time speaking to an audience. Did I mention that I too have the most common fear of public speaking? Yes, that's right, I do. However, I found that once I started speaking all those fears subsided, and it became about the heart of the message and not what the audience thought of me.

I read once that if you are fearful to speak, it's a pride issue because you are making it about you instead of the message. I would like to think that most speakers who are talking about God are doing so because God has laid a message on their hearts. Also, the audience wants the speaker to be successful, and they want to benefit from the message. So, friend, let me encourage you: if you've got a message to share, go do the thing in fear and trembling. God's got you!

I want to give you the same information I shared with that first group of ladies. Over the years many have told me how it has helped them in the mornings. And I believe it's more relevant today than even a few years ago as the world spins faster and faster and our time becomes our most important commodity. Some would argue that time is not the most important commodity, but ask any working or stay-at-home, mom, grandma, aunt, sister, or other woman drawing breath, and I bet she would agree that her time is very important. I believe time is the most valuable thing to most of us.

What would it look like to be able to spend time with God before taking on your day simply by incorporating this precious, God-focused time into your morning routine?

I want to give you some practical tools that have helped me during my busiest seasons in life. Some tools to help you spend time with God when you don't have time to spend with God. However, before we go any further, let's look at the importance of your relationship with God through His Son—Jesus Christ.

> But God proves His own love for us in that while we were still sinners, Christ died for us! (Romans 5:8 NRSV)

Jesus didn't have to come to earth and die to save us, but He did. God's love for us is so great that He gave His only Son to die for us (John 3:16). We are all broken and have been disobedient to God, although we may not realize our sin or brokenness. Let me ask you: Have you ever noticed that you don't have to show a toddler how to misbehave? It's a natural inclination to disobey—to be stubborn or rebellious. It's called the human condition.

Once you realize your sin, then it's time to ask for forgiveness and accept the gift of salvation Jesus Christ offers. It's that simple. You cannot attend enough church services or do enough charitable acts of kindness to go to heaven. And if you could, it would completely disregard the very reason Jesus Christ came and died.

I think we forget this sometimes as we look around at seemingly good people who are doing amazing things to help people, and we think, *I wonder if God will let them into heaven.* Particularly when we see people who are kind-hearted and charitable. There are some amazing folks out there who do so much to help other people. We wonder if it's necessary to have had a salvation experience and a relationship with Jesus Christ to go to heaven. Well, thank goodness and the good Lord, we don't make the rules, and we are not God. I know my judgement would be clouded at best.

Matthew's gospel tells us in chapter 4, verse 17 that Jesus said, "Repent of your sins and turn to God, for the Kingdom of Heaven is near." Forgiveness of sins and turning to God is necessary for heaven. Don't wait around on this; take care of it today by asking God to forgive your sins and accept the gift of salvation that is waiting for you.

Now, dear sister, let's move on to the start of each day with God. Before we do, I want to share the song that inspired me to write this book. Some of you might remember Dionne Warwick's 1967 song "I Say a Little Prayer." The lyrics go like this:

> The moment I wake up
> Before I put on my makeup
> I say a little prayer for you
> While combing my hair, now
> And wondering what dress to wear, now
> I say a little prayer for you
> Forever, forever, you'll stay in my heart
> And I will love you.[1]

"Before I put on my makeup, I say a little prayer for you." This is the heart of the message here, and I can't wait to share more with you.

I was also inspired by an article that I found in my grandma Rivers's Bible from 1975. The article is titled "Makeup Kit." It was written by Edgar R. Cooper and printed in the *Florida Baptist Witness*. Mr. Cooper had the idea to write an article about a lady's makeup kit. I love what Mr. Cooper writes and how it still rings true today. The times have changed a bit, but the message has not changed much at all.

> We went to a friend's home to pick up a relative.
> The lady was planning to spend a few days with

us. In preparation for the journey to our house, the guest-to-be headed for a bedroom saying, "I must get my makeup kit." Today's woman is horrified at the thought of appearing in public as she naturally looks. The Almighty just hasn't done a good enough job. So to keep a lady happy, she must have an assortment of cosmetics—rouge, lipstick, fingernail polish, eyebrow pencil, mascara, false eyelashes, astringents, powder, oils, salves, perfumes, hair spray, deodorant, wigs, molds and most anything else they think will help make them acceptable to the neighbors.[2]

Mr. Cooper goes on to say that there is another kind of makeup kit we all need that deals with the inside of a person rather than the outside. And I completely agree. His article inspired me to dig a little deeper and use cosmetic and skin-care tools that correlate with today's standard of beauty.

Consider doing this while putting on your foundation. Think about the fact that God is your foundation. God and His Word are the very foundation upon which our faith stands. While you are putting on your foundation, praise God for being your foundation and for being God. He is worthy of all your praise, and He is the foundation of your faith. Before you tell me that you don't use foundation, think about something you put on your face every morning. It may be a skin-care product such as a moisturizer. I did a Facebook poll and discovered ten out of eleven women apply a moisturizer or makeup on their face before leaving the house each day.

In the following pages, I will share how to use physical beauty tools as a reminder to use spiritual tools to help us connect and grow in our relationship with God.

What do you think?

Could you use a few tools to start your day with God?

Will you join me?

# Chapter 2

## Jezebel and Influence

Ahab son of Omri did what was evil in the Lord's sight, even
more than any of the kings before him. And as though it
were not enough to follow the sinful example of Jeroboam,
he married Jezebel, the daughter of King Ethbaal of the
Sidonians, and he began to bow down in worship of Baal.
—1 Kings 16:30–31 (NLT)

God warned the Israelites not to marry foreign women because
they would turn them away from Him and influence them to
follow other gods. It wasn't that God didn't love all people. He loves
every person created and desires all to follow Him. It's just that He
knows the hearts of men and how easily they can be influenced by
women. It goes way back to the beginning in Genesis with Adam
and Eve. Eve influenced her husband to eat from the tree that God
had forbidden. Adam had a choice and chose to listen to Eve, and
we all know that's how sin started.

Scripture tell us that King Solomon was deeply attached and loved
his seven hundred wives and three hundred concubines. He allowed
his wives to seduce him into following other gods. It turns out that he
was not as completely devoted to Yahweh his God as his father, King
David. Interestingly, Solomon had just built the temple and dedicated
it to the Lord when the Lord appeared to Solomon a second time.

The LORD said to him:

> I have heard your prayer and petition you have
> made before Me. I have consecrated this temple
> you have built, to put My name there forever; My
> eyes and My heart will be there at all times. As for
> you, if you walk before Me as your father David
> walked, with a heart of integrity and in what is
> right, doing everything I have commanded you,
> and if you keep My statutes and ordinances, I will
> establish your royal throne over Israel forever, as
> I promised your father David: You will never fail
> to have a man on the throne of Israel. If you or
> your sons turn away from following Me and do
> not keep My commands—My statutes that I have
> set before you—and if you go and serve other gods
> and worship them, I will cut off Israel from the
> land I gave them, and I will reject the temple I
> have sanctified for My name. Israel will become an
> object of scorn and ridicule among all the peoples.
> (1 Kings 9:3–7 HCSB)

King Solomon's half-hearted devotion to the Lord became
evident in the way he was influenced and persuaded to allow other
gods to be worshipped. The Lord was angry with Solomon. In
1 Kings 11, God tells him that He will tear the kingdom away,
but not completely because of a promise made to David. Solomon
died in 930 BC after serving as Israel's king for forty years. His
kingdom passed on to his son, Rehoboam. After both Solomon and
Rehoboam failed to be an instrument of justice for their people, the
kingdom split with Israel's kingdom being to the north and Judah's
kingdom being to the south. Fast forward approximately two dozen
kings and fifty-six years, we find ourselves in the story of King Ahab
and Jezebel.

King Ahab reigned over Israel in Samaria for twenty-one years, from 874 to 853 BC. Ahab comes from the lineage of David. David was the one after God's own heart, and he sinned greatly against God. However, the thing I like about David is the way he repents of his sin and pours out his heart to God. The generations after David, including Ahab, soon forgot who God was to those previous generations.

Jezebel was a Phoenician princess, the daughter of Ethbaal, who was king of the Sidonians. The Sidonians were known to worship Baal, who was one of the seven princes of Hell. Jezebel had great influence over her husband, King Ahab. He allowed Baal worship to become prevalent in Israel.

Scripture tells us in 1 Kings 16:32–33 (HCSB) that he set up an altar for Baal in the temple of Baal that he had built in Samaria. Ahab also made an Asherah pole. Ahab did more to provoke the LORD God of Israel than all the kings of Israel who were before him.

At one point, Jezebel ordered that prophets of the Lord be killed and then proceeded to taunt Elijah. This is surprising that Jezebel could taunt Elijah, a prophet of God, who performed wondrous miracles resulting in the deaths of hundreds of prophets of Baal.

Later, when Jezebel heard her husband testify of the miracles God performed and how Elijah had killed the Baal prophets, she became enraged. She sent Elijah running for his life as he hid in a cave, but eventually it would be Jezebel who would paint her face and die a horrible death.

Did you catch that? Jezebel painted her face. Her appearance was so important to her that she put on eye makeup and arranged her hair before standing in the window waiting for Jehu to arrive.

She had heard of Jehu and referred to him as a murderer as he entered the gates of Jezreel. This seems funny coming from someone who had over four hundred prophets of the Lord put to death. Second Kings 9 tells us that Jehu was appointed king of Israel and was ordered to avenge the deaths of the prophets and servants by killing the house of Ahab, and this included Jezebel.

When Jehu arrived, he looked up at the window and asked, "Who is on my side?" The scripture tells us that Jezebel's own eunuchs threw her out of the window, and she fell to her death and was trampled by horses. Jehu ordered she be buried because she was the daughter of a king, but the dogs ate her before they could bury her.

What a crazy story and the evil that existed in the heart of Jezebel. I don't believe for a minute that kind of evil exists in my fellow sisters in Christ. However, this does make me reflect on the reasons why we wear makeup.

Why do we wear makeup and fix our face before leaving the house? Whether it be makeup or moisturizer, most all of us do something to our appearance before going out in public. Let's take a minute and think about …

Am I doing it to be presentable?

Am I doing it to be acceptable to someone else?

Am I more concerned with how others view me?

Am I doing it for me?

I don't believe the reasons above are inherently wrong, but I do think a healthy Christ-centered view of self is important. Understanding that God gives us an innate care for our appearance is valuable and helpful when reaching others. If we put too much emphasis on self, we can fall short, and if we don't care enough about self, we can fall short.

To be honest, this is my struggle. I tend to care too much about my appearance, and it gets on my own nerves. I have always been cute, or at least that's what I was told. I think sometimes short people are called cute because they are short people. I don't know for sure but I'm a whole five feet one, and I'm short, a.k.a. vertically challenged. When I was a teen, I wanted to be considered beautiful but never felt that I was beautiful until years later. I'll share more about this in another chapter.

A healthy view of self is vital to the work God has for you. Do you know that you are influential? Do you understand that your influence in your home, community, and workplace is huge! History reminds us of numerous women who have influenced their husbands and children to do God's work.

Women have been right by the side of Jesus when He walked the earth and were the first to find the empty tomb when He was resurrected. God showed the value of women the very moment He made the virgin Mary pregnant with Jesus. He chose a woman to bring our Lord and Savior into the world and never slowed down using women in the process of following Him and sharing His life since then.

You are vital to the work the Lord is doing in the here and now. Do you believe it?

Do you understand your power and influence over the very household you oversee? What about your community and workplace? The Lord has entrusted this to you, and sometimes we become so consumed with where God wants to use us that we miss the very spot He has put us in.

Why do we think we have to have this huge presence or platform in the world to be important? It's simply a lie from the enemy. Be present where you are, and let God use you in your sphere of influence. No one can influence your family, workplace, or community like you can right where you are in this moment. If God moves you to a bigger platform, then go! If He doesn't, then stay, and do the thing right where you are right now. When God opens doors, no one can shut them, and when God closes doors, no one can open them.

What is your sphere of influence?

Who has God strategically placed in your life?

What doors have remained open by God that you have not walked through?

# Chapter 3

## Esther and Great Faith

*During the year before each young woman's turn to go to
King Ahasuerus, the harem regulation required her to receive
beauty treatments with oil of myrrh for six months and then
with perfumes and cosmetics for another six months.*
—Esther 2:12 (HCSB)

Queen Esther was a Jewish girl who endured much for the good
of her people, and it was a long hard road to get there. You
see, there was another queen before Esther and because she would
not obey the commands of the king, she would be killed, and a
replacement would be needed to hold the position of queen.

Soon a search began for a new queen, and it was an intense
process. Many young virgin women joined wanting to be queen.
Women were not valued at that time, and their only hope to
having success in life depended on a man, and in this case, the
man was a king. If she was picked, there was a good chance she
wouldn't want for anything and neither would her family. So
sending your virgin daughter to the king to do with what the
king's court wanted was an easy decision for the girls and their
families. Plus, I'm not sure how much choice they had in the
matter because all the young virgins were gathered and sent to
the palace.

These young women received several months of beauty treatments. This may sound nice at first, but when we stop to think about the cleansings, plucking and removal of body hair, and procedures to lighten the skin and remove blemishes, it sounds painful. Not to say that it isn't painful for us these days because it certainly can be. However, we have advanced tools to help alleviate the pain, making it more pain-free than ever before. I'm trying to imagine what it was like to have skin lightening procedures and removal of blemishes. I don't know about you, but I would opt for a skincare regimen to take care of skin lightening or removal of blemishes. They were also required to paint their faces with makeup and perfume their bodies.

One by one the young women were presented to King Ahasuerus. They would go to him in the evening, and she would be given whatever she requested to take with her from the palace. In the morning she would return to where the concubines were residing. She would never go to the king again unless he desired her and summoned her by name.

Let's pause here for a minute to reflect on what these girls may have gone through emotionally. It seems they were young—probably in their teens. I'm trying to imagine them being scared to go be with a man for the first time and especially the king.

Do you suppose there was pressure on them to perform?

How do you suppose they felt if the king never summoned them again?

Sadly, these girls were convinced this was their only option for a meaningful life, and there was great competition among women to have the king's favor.

Because Esther was Jewish, she was put in a position of greater sacrifice than most of the other women. She was forced to eat certain foods she would never be able to eat and to have sexual relations with a man who was not her husband.

And even so Esther had a little bit of an advantage because she was taken to the palace and placed under the care of Hegai, who was in-charge of the women. Scripture tells us that she won the king's favor because she didn't request anything except what Hegai suggested.

Esther had a way of winning people over, and she won approval in the sight of everyone who saw her (Esther 2:15). The king was pleased and loved Esther more than all the other women and placed the royal crown on her head and made her queen.

Esther's uncle Mordecai had been instrumental in helping her find her place as queen. Previously, he had taken her into his home from an early age after the deaths of her parents and was very influential in her life.

One day after his niece became the queen, he overheard two guards talking about killing the king and reported it to Esther. She told the king on Mordecai's behalf, and the two guys were hanged. This would prove to be beneficial to the Jewish people later.

One day King Ahasuerus honored a man named Haman and promoted him, giving him a higher position than all the other officials. The king commanded the entire royal staff at the King's Gate to bow and pay homage to Haman. However, Mordecai would not bow down due to his religious principles. He saw Haman as a wicked man full of pride and envy. Honoring such a man is not God-honoring, and even though Mordecai's friends tried to persuade him to bow to Haman, he refused day after day. This enraged Haman!

Haman began a plan to hang Mordecai and destroy all of Mordecai's people—the Jewish people. He told the king there was this ethnic group scattered in every province of the kingdom living in isolation. He said their laws are different and they do not obey the king. He went on to say that it is not in the king's best interest to tolerate them, so the king gave authorization to Haman to do what he saw fit.

While Haman was planning this scheme, the king had a restless night and realized that he had not honored the man who saved his life. The king told Haman about his wishes to honor a man. Haman believes the honor was for him, so he suggests a royal garment that the king had worn be placed on the man and one of the king's horses be used for the person as they parade him through the city square. The king likes that idea and tells him to do that for Mordecai the Jew.

Haman is overwhelmed that Mordecai is the one to be honored, and Haman's family knows he is destined to fall. As the story goes, Esther shares Haman's plans with the king to destroy all the Jewish people starting with Mordecai, the man the king had just honored. Then Haman is hanged on the very gallows he built for Mordecai.

Was it all worth it? God used Esther and gave her favor with the king to save the Jewish people. We don't see God's name written in the book of Esther, but we do see His fingerprints all over it. Esther was beautiful both inside and out and seemed to understand she had a bigger purpose. She sacrificed and endure much not knowing how it would turn out.

Are we willing to be used by God when we don't understand the purpose?

When we prepare ourselves to go to work or go out for the day, do we consider our appearance for God, or do we even give it a thought?

What would it look like to think about our appearance from a godly point of view?

You are a cherished daughter of King Jesus. The One who loves you more than you can imagine and gave His life for you. Maybe we should start thinking differently about our appearance and consider what is attractive to God.

We are to be witnesses for Jesus Christ and help others to see Jesus and follow Him. How you present yourself is vital, and it starts with a first impression in our appearance. After that, it's all about the heart. People will know if we care about them by the words that pour out of our mouths: "For the mouth speaks from the overflow of the heart" (Matthew 12:34).

My sister in Christ, let's give some thought to our appearance.

Not from the perspective of what I can gain but what can Christ gain through me.

What can you do to your appearance today that honors God?

How will you reflect the light of Christ?

Are you willing to submit to being used by God even when you don't feel like it or understand the purpose?

# Chapter 4

## Eye of the Beholder

For God so loved the world that he gave his one and only Son,
that whoever believes in him shall not perish but have eternal life.
—John 3:16 (NIV)

God loves you!

Honestly how many times in your life have you heard that? Probably a lot! It may be overused, but it doesn't make it any less true.

God loves and adores you.

He gave His one and only Son for you.

A popular scripture says,

> For God so loved the world that he gave his one and
> only Son, that whoever believes in him shall not
> perish but have eternal life. (John 3:16 NIV)

God was thinking of me and you when He sent His one and only Son to die for us. We live in an imperfect world and are born with sin that needs redeeming. The only way to redeem our sin is to believe in Jesus Christ who died for our sin.

I love what Romans 10:9–10 (HCSB) says about salvation.

If you confess with your mouth, "Jesus is Lord," and believe in your heart that God raised Him from the dead, you will be saved. One believes with the heart, resulting in righteousness, and one confesses with the mouth, resulting in salvation.

This is good news!

God knit you together in your mother's womb and loves you more than you could ever imagine. The only comparison I begin to make is when I became a mother. You give birth to a little person you carried inside you for months, and the moment you see your baby, you are madly in love.

You are likely in love with your baby before birth, but for sure when you see your baby. This is also true of moms who adopt their baby. They want their little one so badly, and sometimes they have wanted and prayed many years before knowing the child was coming to them. We love our babies to the ends of the earth, and it doesn't matter if they are pretty or not so pretty babies, we see them as beautiful! How is that possible?

Could it be that we develop a relationship with someone unseen? We fall in love because we know there is a little baby coming who will bless us and depend on us for all its needs. Hmm, could it be the same for us in our relationship with God? We've never seen God, yet He created us and takes care of all our needs. We don't always know how God provides and takes care of us or how He protects us from harm. He is constantly watching over us and loving us.

I wonder how Mary felt when she gave birth to Jesus. When she went into labor, do you think she had a clue what was about to happen? Did she really understand her emotional state of mind and the hormones she experienced while pregnant and giving birth? I believe, because she was fully human and experiencing childbirth, it was much like we experience (except He was and is the Son of God).

I'm trying to imagine the shepherds showing up to see Jesus when He was born and telling Mary and Joseph about the multitude of angels that appeared to them to tell them about the birth of their little baby, who is the Christ. Luke 2:19 tells us Mary was treasuring all these things in her heart and meditating on them.

Fast forward many years, and we find Mary asking Jesus to perform His first miracle of turning water into wine at a wedding. He would try to tell her that it was not His time yet, but He went on to perform the miracle anyway. This was to display His glory and for His disciples to believe in Him. I also wonder if He was being respectful and loving to His mother by doing what she asked of Him. The Old Testament law says to honor your father and mother. And Jesus came to fulfill the law, not abolish it. He knew this act of obedience would honor His mother, and even though it was not His time yet, He would go to perform His first public miracle. Jesus knew the heart of His mother in making this request, and He loved and honored His mother.

There are numerous stories of Jesus seeing right to the heart of people. He can see us in ways we are not able to see ourselves. He loves us in such a way that we are beautiful in His eyes.

Take the story of the woman at the well. Jesus was a Jew, and the woman at the well was a Samaritan. It wasn't appropriate for Him to speak to her, yet He held a conversation with her telling her things that no one else would know (John 4). He saw right through to her heart and told her not to sin any longer and told her in such a way that made her feel beautiful and not ashamed.

There's something about feeling valued and being disciplined at the same time. It's a lost art in this day and time. But Jesus did that with everyone He encountered and is our example. He was able to value and cherish the person in front of Him even though He may have been telling the individual about his or her sin. He loves all and sees all from a perspective of adoration and love and views each created person with incredible beauty.

What about the story of the woman who was disabled for eighteen years? She was bent over and could not straighten up at all (Luke 13). Jesus said, "Woman, you are free of your disability," and then He laid His hands on her and instantly she was restored and began to glorify God. Jesus was criticized by the leader of the synagogue for performing this miracle on the Sabbath.

*Matthew Henry's Commentary* explains this story in more detail.

She is a daughter of Abraham, in a relation to whom you all pride yourselves; she is your sister, and shall she be denied a favor that you grant to an ox or an ass, dispensing a little with the supposed strictness of the Sabbath day? She is a daughter of Abraham and therefore is entitled to the Messiah's blessings—to the bread that belongs to the children. She is one whom Satan has bound. He had a hand in the affliction, and therefore it was not only an act of charity to the poor woman but of piety to God, to break the power of the devil and baffle him. She has been in this deplorable condition, lo, these eighteen years, and therefore, now that there is an opportunity of delivering her, it ought not to be deferred a day longer, as you would have it, for any of you would have thought eighteen years of affliction full long enough.

She was a daughter of Abraham, and we are too! Jesus couldn't watch this eighteen-year-old woman suffer a day more. He was trying to tell the leader of the synagogue that she is your sister in the faith. He saw her, and He sees you!

He sees your suffering.

He sees your grief.

He sees your medical condition.

He sees your financial burden.

He sees your heartache.

He sees your loneliness.

He sees your concerns over your children.

Most of all ...

He sees your heart.

And He loves you.

He really loves you.

Jesus sees what you are going through and what is on your heart. He knows, and He loves you. I believe He wants to bring healing to the very place that is troubling you most.

I pray you have people in your life that love you when you wake up and when you go to bed and every moment in between. I also hope you know the God who does behold you. He doesn't care if you have showered, put on makeup, or have the most stylish clothes. He loves you for you! I hope you have submitted your life to Christ and understand just how precious you are to Him.

If beauty really is in the eye of the beholder, then who is beholding you?

Who are you beholding?

Do you understand just how much Christ loves you?

# Chapter 5

## Jars of Clay

Now we have this treasure in clay jars, so that this
extraordinary power may be from God and not from us.
We are pressured in every way but not crushed; we are
perplexed but not in despair; we are persecuted but not
abandoned; we are struck down but not destroyed.
—2 Corinthians 4:7–9 (HCSB)

Life is hard, and sometimes it seems too hard. We are fragile,
imperfect beings yet strong enough to endure pressure,
persecution, and being struck down. How is it possible to be so
weak and yet so strong? How can a weak and imperfect vessel be
able to endure hard things?

Whether you are a Christ follower or not, life happens.
Life happens to all of us, and some think that when we become
Christians, life should be easy, but that's not what the Bible tells us
in 2 Corinthians 4.

Paul is writing to the Corinthian church to encourage them of
the extraordinary power they have during times of pressure, despair,
and persecution. He explains that our perfect God has chosen to
make His sanctuary in the lives of unworthy sinners, like you and
me. We are jars of clay—imperfect vessels—designed out of the dust

of the earth to live a life glorifying God. We have this treasure within us, and it is the extraordinary power from God.

No matter how shiny and clean we appear on the outside, many of us are suffering with afflictions. We are pressured but not crushed; we are perplexed but not in despair; we are persecuted but not abandoned, and we are struck down but not destroyed.

Pressured, struck down, and persecuted are what Jesus experienced while walking on this earth. As a result, when we follow Jesus, we experience much of the same. I don't know why we are surprised when suffering comes. Suffering always comes, and yet we don't want to suffer. When suffering comes, we can endure because of the strength found in Jesus Christ. God gives us the power of the Holy Spirit to guide, direct, protect, instruct, and support. And when we endure suffering for Jesus and think we can't take it any longer, the extraordinary power of God illuminates the way.

I've found that when suffering comes, these are the moments I feel closest to God. God hears our cries for Him and rushes in to help us get through times of suffering and despair. Psalm 34:18 says, "The Lord is close to the broken-hearted and saves those who are crushed in spirit."

Many people have suffered without knowing or understanding why. I too have experienced this in my life. I grew up having epilepsy, and it was never a fun experience having seizures and taking antiseizure medication. The first seizure happened at age four when my mom found me unconscious on the floor. On the way to the hospital in the ambulance, I remember the conversations being said about me as I looked down on my body riding in the ambulance. I recall the paramedics having a conversation with my mom asking which hospital and the name of my doctor. Years later, I would ask my mom if this is what I heard, and she confirmed it happened exactly that way.

I suffered with epilepsy until I was a teen. It was scary to think that I could have a seizure at school or in front of friends. I told a teacher in grade school, and she tried to fail me. My dad went to see the teacher and discuss why she wanted to hold me back when I was making good grades. She explained that "with Kim's condition, I thought it would be best." Of course, my dad helped her see she was wrong. On another occasion, I told a friend, and she proceeded to make fun of me, so I learned very quickly *not* to tell anyone. This made me feel isolated and alone.

I took medication to control the seizures, which is a story in itself. The pills were huge capsules, and I had to learn how to swallow them starting at four years old. One pill didn't control the seizures, so I had to take two pills. That didn't control the seizures either, so I had to take three pills a day until I was thirteen years old. I went in often for EEGs (electroencephalogram) to detect any abnormalities in my brain waves, which evaluates the electrical activity in my brain. This helped the doctors determine when I could start weaning off the medicine.

I had petit mal seizures, and with my form of epilepsy, many children outgrow them, and that was the case for me. I am so grateful that as my brain developed, I outgrew the seizures and was able to stop the medication. To this day, though, I don't know why I went through that as a child.

There are many forms of suffering. Ask believers how they take the next step after the death of a spouse or a parent who loses a child, and they will tell you it's one step at a time. Often, they can't see a future because their grief is so severe. However, they have hope of a future with their loved one that spurs them on to the next day. Slowly, they learn how to live a new normal without their loved one.

Same goes for those who are suffering from an illness or watching a loved one suffer. It's debilitating and frustrating when you need answers, and yet they don't come. We continue to move forward with prayer because we know our hope comes from the Lord. Sometimes healing comes here and sometimes in heaven. We may or may not have answers, and this leaves us perplexed.

Sometimes we are perplexed and uncertain about our current situation or future. The disciples felt this when they were being persecuted and were in doubt of what would become of them. We are not all that different. I know many women who are searching for God's will in their lives. They keep asking how God wants to use them and seem uncertain or confused about the direction. I went through this too at one point in my life and found that being available to God right where He placed me was the answer. God opens doors that no one can close, and He will close doors that no one can open. Be confident where God has placed you in the here and now. If you are to do more or have a bigger calling or platform, it will happen. God doesn't need us to manipulate the thing to get to where we are going. If we do, sometimes we are not ready for it, and God will put us where we belong. I have literally been working on this book for years and don't understand why it's taking so long, but it is all about God's timing and not mine.

Persecution and pressure come in a variety of ways, and social media is just one way many feel persecuted or pressured. It's easy for people to hide behind posts and say things that they would never say to your face. People will say mean things and argue online, battling it out in front of everyone. No one ever wins in these battles, and I'm pretty sure no one has won a soul for Jesus in this way. I think we've forgotten that the battle is about souls and not about who is right.

We are broken people, patched up to be used for God's purposes just like a jar of clay. Inside this jar of clay is a treasure, and it's God's light. This light of Christ that shines through our weakness and brokenness is meant to illuminate the darkness. We are meant to extinguish the darkness and be a shining light for Jesus.

Paul goes on to finish the chapter in verses 17–18:

> For our light and momentary troubles are achieving
> for us an eternal glory that far outweighs them all.
> So we fix our eyes not on what is seen, but on what
> is unseen, since what is seen is temporary, but what
> is unseen is eternal.

Our troubles may not seem light or momentary to us, but we trust the scriptures when it tells us that eternal glory far outweighs them all. Let's fix our eyes not on what is seen but what is unseen, because we have been commissioned to share the eternal truth and hope found in Jesus, our Lord and Savior.

How are you being pressured, perplexed, or persecuted?

How can your suffering help others?

Where do you need healing so you can shine a light for Christ?

# Chapter 6

## Tools for Your Spiritual Makeup Bag

Zillah also gave birth to Tubal-Cain, the ancestor of
blacksmiths and all artisans of bronze and iron.
—Genesis 4:22 (CEB)

I can tell you from experience that my day goes much better when I
first spend time with God before I do anything to my appearance.
Only God can work from the inside out and can only work if we
allow Him. Please consider putting God first in your day. If you are
not able to spend time in the Bible each morning, then your mind
is not set on the things of Christ. So how about some spiritual tools
to help you get started? Guess what? They are right in your makeup
bag. Let's explore them.

Did you know that a person by the name of Tubal-Cain created
tools as weapons in Genesis?

Zillah also gave birth to Tubal-Cain, the ancestor of blacksmiths
and all artisans of bronze and iron.

From the beginning, God has been giving us tools we need for
life. Tubal-Cain created bronze tools and weapons out of copper and
tin. Like the tools he built as weapons, we have tools right in our
makeup bag to help us use as spiritual weapons.

26

## Spiritual Makeup Bag Tools

The first tool in your spiritual makeup bag is foundation. Whether you use a cream, liquid, or powder foundation, most of us use foundation of some sort when applying makeup.

> In the beginning, Lord, you laid the foundation of the earth and made the heavens with your hands. (Hebrews 1:10)

> Righteousness and justice are the foundation of your throne. Unfailing love and truth walk before you as attendants. (Psalm 89:14)

Foundation = Praising God

God created the earth by laying the foundation for us, and remembering who He is and praising Him is a wonderful start. God deserves to be praised first and adored for who He is and what He has done for us. While putting on your makeup and applying your foundation, praise God.

First Peter 3:5 says to praise God because of the promise that those who put their hope in God are beautiful in His sight. God looks upon your heart, so praise Him. After all He formed you in your mother's womb just like He did Jeremiah. You are His beautiful creation, precious in His sight, and He knows you better than you know yourself. He is worthy of all praise.

I must tell you that it makes sense to have a spiritual makeup bag. Wouldn't it be something if we started with the inside each morning instead of the outside. What would our day look like?

Remember the line Rene Zellweger said in the movie *Jerry McGuire,* to Tom Cruise when he arrives at the house and interrupts the ladies to tell her he wants her back. Rene said, "You had me at hello."

God has had you from the beginning of your life and loves you more than you can fathom. God has had you from your very "hello" moment when He created you. You are the very apple of His eye. He wants you to come to Him and realize that He is your God and to praise Him for it. Once you realize and accept this truth, praise becomes your foundation in your relationship with God.

Just like foundation is the first thing in place before anything structural, so is it with praise. God wants to be invited into the beginning of our day. Spending time with God first thing in the morning is best, and while you are putting on your foundation, praise God for who He is and what He has done for you. You may do this by speaking words of praise to God. Listening to praise music or the audio Bible are just a few ways you can invite God into your morning routine with praise.

Perfume/Body Wash = Confession

Confession and repentance are necessary tools to be in a right relationship with God. Simply inviting Jesus into your life and asking Him for forgiveness of sin is the key to salvation and eternal life with God.

> If you confess with your mouth, "Jesus is Lord," and
> believe in your heart that God raised Him from the
> dead, you will be saved. (Romans 10:9)

A daily time of confession is important to keep communication clear with God. Ask God to forgive you where you have not walked in His way or lived according to His Word. I believe God considers confession a sweet fragrance much like perfume. There's nothing sweeter to our Savior than a child coming to confess to Him. Once confession has taken place, then repentance will also change our appearance from the inside out. To turn the heart from sin and self does more for us than changing the color of our lipstick. The loveliness of God shines on our faces. When you put on perfume, confess to God where you have fallen short and repent. This is a sweet fragrance to our Lord.

Now He uses us to spread the knowledge of Christ everywhere, like a sweet perfume. Our lives are a Christlike fragrance rising to God. But this fragrance is perceived differently by those who are being saved and by those who are perishing (2 Corinthians 2:14–15).

I must tell you about something interesting that happens from time to time. I believe I smell the presence of God, and I tend to think it's the Holy Spirit. Now there is nothing biblical about smelling God, so this is just my opinion and experience. There have been occasions when I have not used perfume, yet a sweet smell would fill an area around me. The first time I noticed it, I was by myself in my closet. On many occasions, I will pray in my closet before I get ready for the day. One day as I was dressing, I smelled this wonderful sweet smell. It happened again one weekend when I had a friend here visiting. When I detected the smell, I ran to her excitedly and asked if she could smell it, and she could. I told her I was sure it was the Holy Spirit.

On another occasion, in a local department store, I was checking out, and the clerk asked me what perfume I was wearing. I had noticed the smell again and was glad she did too. I told her that I was not wearing perfume and that I thought it was "the presence of God." She didn't even flinch and said she thought that was cool. I felt sure she would have me escorted out of the store.

As I did some research on fragrance, I found 2 Corinthians 2:14–15 and came to believe that God was simply spreading the knowledge of Christ everywhere like a sweet perfume. I'm honored that He thought He could use this vessel to share the fragrance of Christ.

Can you imagine the sweet fragrance of believers around the

world sharing Christ? Oh, dear sister, I can imagine! Keep your heart in line with God, confess your sins often, and allow the fragrance of Christ to fill and surround you.

## Brush = Forgiveness

> He is so rich in kindness and grace that he purchased our freedom with the blood of his Son and forgave our sins. (Ephesians 1:7)

Understanding God's forgiveness and having a personal relationship with Christ allows us an opportunity to forgive others. When we truly understand our own forgiveness, then it's easier to forgive others.

A tool to remind us of forgiveness would be a brush. When we use a cosmetic brush or hairbrush, we are brushing away any bitterness or unforgiveness. Remember, our first step is knowing that God as our foundation. Once we have recognized who God is and confessed, we would seal the praise and confession with the act of giving forgiveness. Forgiveness works in a way that allows the heart and soul to mend.

When we apply forgiveness to others, we are brushing away any loose particles that creep into the crevices of our hearts. When we don't brush those things away, they settle in our hearts, and an attitude of bitterness can rise. This reflects on our faces and hair if we don't brush these things off, and eventually bitterness and unforgiveness clumps up in our heart, which blocks us from being the daughters of God we are meant to be.

It's not always easy to forgive, as some hurts are very deep. Ask God to soften your heart toward the matter, and make it a daily practice to ask God to help you forgive. I heard someone speak about this recently, and she stated that the act of forgiving is a process. It can be hard to say you forgive someone and then just be over it. It starts when you speak of forgiving someone even when you don't feel like it and asking God to help you walk toward forgiveness every day. She said eventually you will find yourself in a place of forgiveness.

Think about this with me for a moment. When we don't use our cosmetic brushes properly, our faces are covered with uneven flaws, and everyone can see them. The same is true with a hairbrush; when we don't brush our hair, it tangles and is a complete mess. It's the same with forgiveness. If we don't offer forgiveness, we carry that around a tangled and clumpy mess and that becomes a reflection of our hearts. So, when you are using your cosmetic brush or hairbrush, ask God to show you areas where you may need forgiveness or to whom you may need to offer forgiveness. Do it quickly in order to have God's best for the day. Jesus offered ultimate forgiveness for you and me, therefore making it possible for us to offer forgiveness to others. And Jesus makes it very clear that if we don't forgive others, we cannot have the forgiveness that we need so badly from God.

Mascara/Accessorizing = Prayer

> Pray at all times in the Spirit with every prayer and request, and stay alert in this with all perseverance and intercession for all the saints. (Ephesians 5:17)

> The LORD has heard my plea for help; the LORD accepts my prayer. (Psalm 6:9)

At this point, you have used tools in your spiritual makeup bag to bring you into right focus with God. You have praised Him, confessed your heart, and sought forgiveness. Now it's time to pray!

I don't know about you, but I seem to have a relationship with my mascara. I love mascara, and sometimes have a problem applying too much. I can get carried away with it! If you don't believe me, just take a gander at some of my high school photos.

If you don't apply mascara, then you probably accessorize by putting on jewelry. Whatever you are doing as a final repetitive step, consider praying while doing it.

While you are applying mascara to your eyelashes or accessorizing for the day, lift your prayers one by one. Consider how God knows each one and hears each prayer. Whether you have only a few lashes or several lashes or whether you have much accessorizing to do or just a little, this time allows you to pray. Sometimes we have several prayers and sometimes only a few.

Prayer reveals our heart and relationship with God and is simply a conversation. In my prayers, I like to include praying for unbelievers, praying for others, and praying for myself.

Keep in mind that it's not necessary to use the makeup tools outlined in this chapter. Consider what you do each day to get ready for the day, and incorporate those tools into your morning routine. You might find chapter 7 helpful for skincare tools instead of makeup tools. Whatever works best for you to spend time with God is the goal. I will say nothing replenishes the soul like time with God while reading your Bible, spending time in prayer, and listening to God in the mornings before taking on your day.

Do you spend time with God each day?

Which beauty tools do you use each day?

Which four tools from your makeup bag would be helpful to start your day with God?

# Chapter 7

## Love the Skin You're In

I will attach tendons to you and make flesh come upon you
and cover you with skin; I will put breath in you, and you
will come to life. Then you will know that I am the Lord.
—Ezekiel 37:6 (NIV)

In the beginning, like the very beginning in Genesis 1:27, God
created man in His own image. He created both male and female,
blessed them and said to be fruitful and multiply. And so, they did.
In the creation of man and woman, God designed us with skin to
cover our bodies to hold our bones and ligaments in place and to
give us covering.

Our skin is the largest organ of the body, making up 15 percent
of our total body weight. It gives us our unique look, and although
two faces may look similar, no two faces are exact and identical. Even
with identical twins, there will be something different to identify
them as unique. Just ask their mother!

Skin is interesting to me and something I struggled with as a
child. I was allergic to my own perspiration and would develop a
rash under my arms and on my feet when I wore closed-toe shoes.
I don't know the exact name of this condition, but it was not fun! I
had many trips to the dermatologist and had to soak my feet every
evening in a special oil. If I didn't, my feet would get red and itchy,

and I would scratch them until they bled. It was gross, and I hated it! I don't have this condition any longer, but I still have sensitive itchy skin, so I do all I can to take care of it.

In the Bible, there is a reference to skin problems. Moses and Aaron had to check people out to see if they had a defiling skin disease. If they did, they had to look like a defiling skin-diseased person and tear their clothes and have unkept hair. They had to holler, "Unclean, unclean!" so that people wouldn't come near them. They also had to live alone and outside the camp. Talk about isolation.

The LORD said to Moses and Aaron, when anyone has a swelling or a rash or a shiny spot on their skin that may be a defiling skin disease, that person must be brought to Aaron the priest or to one of his sons who is a priest. People with such a defiling disease must wear torn clothes, let their hair be unkempt, cover the lower part of their faces and cry out, "Unclean! Unclean!" As long as they have the disease, they remain unclean. They must live alone; they must live outside the camp (Leviticus 13:1, 45–46).

How terrible for those who suffered with skin problems. Can you even imagine what that would be like these days? We are so consumed with our rights for all kinds of reasons, but to think of what this must have been like for those who were suffering, I simply cannot imagine.

Fortunately, today we don't have to live in isolation when we have skin issues. We can simply go the dermatologist, and many of our skin ailments are cured or, at the very least, treated.

A few years ago, I made the decision to join a skincare company as a consultant representing their products. I am having a blast as I see my skin aging backward and helping others do the same. I have always taken good care of my skin, or at least I thought I was, but it was more cosmetic in nature and not really changing the way my skin acts and feels. I'm loving my skin, which is something you don't normally hear at my age, and I am becoming more comfortable in my skin and loving the results.

For my friends who don't wear makeup, let's discuss steps you could incorporate into your routine to reflect your relationship with God while using a skincare regimen. Here are my suggestions as you wash and care for your face.

## Step One: Cleansing Mask/Face Wash = Praise God

This is a first step as you begin your skincare regimen, and while doing so remember that God is the first step in your day. Praise God that He is the very beginning of your life yesterday, today, and tomorrow. Just like washing your face or using a mask to draw impurities from your face, know that God is first and foremost in your life. He deserves to be recognized as your first today, so praise Him, and by applying the first step in your skincare routine, remember that God is your first and deserves all praise and glory. Recognize who He is and what He has done for you while you apply the first step of your regimen, and remember to praise Him because He is God!

## Step Two: Toner/Body Wash = Confession

When applying toner, you are balancing pH levels in your face that are necessary to prepare your skin for steps three and four. Without toner, your skin does not want to accept the next steps, so it's imperative that you use toner.

If you don't use toner, it may be easier to consider something else that reminds you of confession such as a body wash when you shower or bathe.

By taking time to confess our sin, this opens a path for communication with God. We don't want our hearts to become clogged with things that get in the way for us to be able to hear from God, and because we don't want that blockage, it's important to take a moment to confess.

Often, I will say something like this: "Father, forgive me for the ways I have not walked according to your will or lived according to your way for my life." I'll take a moment to hear from God to know what I need to confess specifically. God speaks to us when we take time to listen. So, while applying your toner to prepare your skin for more or using your body wash, be sure to apply confession to prepare your heart for more.

## Step Three: Skin Treatment/Moisturizer = Forgiveness

While applying step three, which could be either the treatment part of the regimen or simply a moisturizer, consider forgiveness. Think about the forgiveness that you need and receive from God and those you need to forgive. You see forgiveness is a salve all by itself. It relieves stress and pressure in relationships both with God and others. There is something healing in forgiveness that allows us to move on and move past just like in step three of a skincare regimen.

The skin is treated or moisturized and able to heal and move on to a better appearance. This is where you start to age backward and where you find freedom to be liberated from a wrong done to you or by you. There is something liberating in forgiveness that you won't find anywhere else.

## Step Four: Sunscreen or Eye Cream/Serum = Prayers

This is the final step of our skincare regimen. In the morning, you apply sunscreen, and at night, you apply eye cream or face serum or maybe both.

To take on the day, you need to protect yourself with sunscreen just like covering yourself and others with prayer. Having time with God in the morning also protects your soul and attitude. When things come against you during the day, you won't let them affect you quite the same way if you've first spent time with God. By filling your mind with God things, you will be protecting your thoughts and attitudes for the day when challenges come. And oh, dear friend, they will come.

In the evening by putting on eye cream, you are covering your eyes with a remedy to help prevent the signs of aging around your eyes. Consider what your eyes have seen all day and pray as you protect the delicate skin around your eyes.

Whether it's morning or evening, you can lift your prayer requests while applying sunscreen or eye cream. Remembering talking to God through prayer is a vital part of your relationship with God. He wants to hear from you so instead of falling asleep while praying, go ahead and pray during this application time.

What will work best for you, using makeup tools or skincare tools?

If it's skincare tools, which ones do you use each day/night?

How can you use your skincare tools in the four steps in this chapter?

# Chapter 8

## Beauty from the Inside Out

Woe to you, scribes and Pharisees, hypocrites! You clean the
outside of the cup and dish, but inside they are full of greed
and self-indulgence! Blind Pharisee! First clean the inside
of the cup, so the outside of it may also become clean.
—Matthew 23:25–26 (HCSB)

Jesus is making a point here in Matthew 23 to illustrate the
obsession with ritual religious purity and the neglect of inner
spiritual purity. The same can be true of our outer appearance as
we forget to take care of our inner beauty. For now, let's look more
closely at the Pharisees.

The Pharisees were thought to be very good men because of their
commitment to religious activity. It would seem on the outside they
did everything right by the way they tithed, served, and followed
religious laws. However, inside, their hearts were corrupt with
wickedness.

We still have Pharisees walking around today. They are not
called Pharisees but Christians. Not all Christians are Pharisees, but
there are some who do practice religion and not relationship. What I
mean by that is some Christians will go to church and serve in their
community with a profound sense of doing it for God. However,

they don't really *know* God by way of His Son, Jesus Christ. It is through Jesus Christ that we have a relationship with God.

It is about a relationship *with* God, not a practice of religion *for* God. Is God okay with religion? I think so, since He created religion. During Old Testament times, God appointed priests to serve in the temple for religious practices such as sacrificing for the sins of the people. Religion itself is not bad, but if you have only religion and not a relationship with God through Jesus, then you are lacking.

We live in New Testament times, meaning we have Jesus Christ as our perfect sacrifice. You see, no amount of service or sacrifice can save you; it is only the saving grace of Jesus Christ that can do that for you. Once you have a relationship with God through Jesus, you will serve with a pure motive, and you will have the Holy Spirit guiding you along the way.

Interestingly, the Pharisees are compared to whitewashed tombs (sepulchers), which appear beautiful on the outside but inside are full of dead men's bones and every impurity (Matthew 23:27). It was Jewish custom to whiten grave tombs for a couple of reasons: to notify people of a grave so a person could avoid touching the grave due to ceremonial pollution, and they were whitened to make them beautiful and appear that the dead persons were righteous. The decoration of a grave such as ornaments, flowers, or dressing up the dead body for show were acts to appear righteous before men. Matthew 6:1 warns us against practicing righteousness in front of people to be seen, or there will be no reward from our Father in heaven.

What does all that mean for us? The world tells us we deserve to take time for ourselves by preparing our outer beauty. As attractive as caring for outer beauty makes us, how much more important is it to spend the time caring for our inner beauty? Inner beauty is what makes the outside beautiful, and Jesus is the way to inner beauty.

When I was thirteen years old at a small church revival in Oklahoma, I walked the aisle to accept Jesus Christ as my Lord and Savior. Although my relationship with Christ started at age thirteen, my walk with the Lord didn't begin until I was thirty-eight years old. That's twenty-five years of having the Holy Spirit and never learning what to do with it. I wasn't discipled to learn how to be a Christ follower. When I started learning what that meant, I started transforming from the inside out.

During those twenty-five years, God watched over me and protected me and was so good to me. I don't understand why other than He is just a good God. My mom prayed for me during those years to come back to the Lord. It wasn't as if I always intentionally strayed, but I did a fair amount.

I would go to church on and off during those years. I would do good things and some not so good things. I was a C&E (Christmas and Easter) Christian and thought that was okay. However, I had a praying mom in the background, and when my sister became old enough, she prayed for me too.

The power of prayer is huge! If you are praying for someone to come to the Lord or come back to the Lord, keep praying. There's no timestamp on prayers. If you are still alive and drawing breath, keep praying. Sister, you may not know how your prayers are in the process of being answered until you are with the Lord, and I've got proof.

My mom also prayed for my son from the time he was born until she passed. He was eight years old when she died. She prayed for two things: his salvation and a Christian wife. His salvation came two weeks after her death. I didn't know she prayed these things until after her death, and my sister shared with me. Think about this for a second. Can you imagine being in heaven with God and Jesus and seeing the angels celebrate your grandson accepting the saving grace of Jesus? She may not have seen her prayer answered here on earth, but she had the best seat in the house in heaven when it did come to fruition. Glory!

When 9/11 occurred, I was thirty-eight years old, and it was an awakening. I realized that I had been playing church. We found a church home, and I quickly dove into the Word. I studied every single day for hours on end. I joined women's Bible study and eventually an evangelistic program to learn how to share the gospel with others. I grew exponentially with the Lord, and during that time, my mom was diagnosed with an illness that would eventually take her life. She saw me come back to the Lord and grow in my walk. This was another answer to her prayers.

My walk with the Lord has changed me to feel beautiful, and I love that about our God. He loves us in such a way that when we follow Him and start to believe it, we feel beautiful. Beauty from the inside out is the best kind of beauty. A beautiful heart leads us to love like God, and this is the thing, from which everything else flows.

Our growing and walking with the Lord never ends while we are here on earth. Through the years, God has given me a love to help other women in their walk with the Lord. That is why I've written this book. If you don't have time to spend with God, then use the tools in your spiritual makeup bag. The more you do this, I'm praying you will become hungrier for more of God, and when that happens, try taking the next step.

Try starting your day with God by reading your Bible or Bible app. Before doing so, pray and ask God to speak to you through His Word. Think about the scriptures and seek understanding for what they mean by using the cross-references in your Bible.

If you are not a part of a Bible-believing church, then start seeking one that places high importance on Jesus and His teachings. Finally, as you spend time with God, I promise you will begin to transform with beauty from the inside out.

My sister in Christ, are you walking with the Lord?

Do you understand your beauty comes from the Lord?

What would the world look like if we allowed God to speak to us and use us for His glory?

Don't try to make yourselves beautiful on the outside, with stylish hair or by wearing gold jewelry or fine clothes. Instead, make yourselves beautiful on the inside, in your hearts, with the enduring quality of a gentle, peaceful spirit. This type of beauty is very precious in God's eyes (1 Peter 3:3–4 CEB).

# Notes

1    Dionne Warwick, Lyrics to *I Say a Little Prayer*, Scepter Records, 1967.
2    1975 Makeup Kit, Edgar R. Cooper, *Florida Baptist Witness*, 14–15.

Printed in the United States
By Bookmasters